DUST RUNNER

poems by

Jessica Jewell

Finishing Line Press
Georgetown, Kentucky

DUST RUNNER

ACKNOWLEDGMENTS

I want to express my gratitude to the editors of the following magazines in which
some of these poems first appeared: *Barn Owl Review, Clark Street Review, Nimrod,
Harpur Palate, Rhino, Soft Blow, Touchstone*

Thank you to the Northeast Ohio Master of Fine Arts, the Wick Poetry Center,
and Kent State University for the time, encouragement, and resources to write and
develop this manuscript, and for your support of my teaching and scholarship.

My sincere thanks to the Wick family, without whose support these poems would
have never found their way to the page. I owe so many landscapes to my stay in
Bisbee, and I will forever be grateful for all that you do for artists.

To my teachers and mentors, Karen Kovacik, Maggie Anderson, Mary Biddinger, and
Craig Paulenich, my sincerest gratitude for everything you've done to help shape my
poems and my writing life.

To my dear friend Lindsay Bennett, without whom this manuscript would likely be
buried under a tumbleweed in Tombstone.

A lifetime of gratitude to my wife, Györgyi Mihályi-Jewell, for her patience and love
and stars and moon.

Publisher: Leah Maines
Editor: Christen Kincaid
Cover Art and Design: Zuzana Kubišova
Author Photo: Györgyi Mihályi-Jewell

Printed in the USA on acid-free paper.
Order online: www.finishinglinepress.com
also available on amazon.com

Author inquiries and mail orders:
Finishing Line Press
P. O. Box 1626
Georgetown, Kentucky 40324
U. S. A.

Table of Contents

For my parents, Rob and Mary Jewell

Author's Note:

By the 1920s, the demand for coal in the United States had fallen drastically, and as a result, many coal mining companies went out of business. In the late fall of 1932, the Cumberland Consolidated Coal Company in Harlan, Kentucky permanently closed. Three hundred and fifty miners scattered with their families, seeking work in one of over one hundred coal camps in Harlan County. Most miners were left jobless, wandering all winter from camp to camp.

Because the economies of the coal camps were wholly dependent upon the companies, those who weren't miners, but were employed in the camps and surrounding towns, were also forced to look for work. Among these people were teachers, doctors, store clerks, and preachers. A few who had the means traveled further west, some as far as the Great Plains, where at one time farming opportunities were abundant.

The people from the Southern Mountains who went as far as Oklahoma discovered a failing land—a land that had greatly suffered from years of over-cultivation and was now entrenched in an extended drought. The result was a near decade of dust storms—"black blizzards." During that awful decade known as the Dust Bowl, some of the population left for California, though nearly two-thirds were either unwilling or unable to abandon their homesteads.

In the process of writing this book, I consulted the following sources: *Letters from the Dust Bowl* by Caroline Henderson; *The Golden Bough* by Sr. James George Frazer; and *American Indian Myths and Legends*, selected and edited by Richard Erdoes and Alfonso Ortiz.

THE FLUTE

Buffalo-robed, the women gathered
fresh water in skin bags, whistled
all afternoon with the yellowlegs
while the men grouped around the fire
and spoke of songs. As sunset neared
the men called down the trilling birds,
asked them to give their bodies for a flute.

In the old days, the birds would oblige,
turn the color of dried nettle, hollow
for the wind song. The next morning,
at the river, one man woke, parted
the grizzly-thick woods to approach
a woman at the bank, now collecting
stones, birch bark, turnips.

We called that the ritual of love, Abigail—
The song in all its sacrifices.

He played for her and she danced circles
around the hemlocks, mud collecting
on the leather ties of her moccasins.

Now, no bird should give her body
for a flute, nor a woman for a song.

Mountains

earth pulled
to where it would not go

—Jean Valentine

MOTHER'S BURIAL, 1920

I saw the mist, white wing,
lift up from the pit in the earth.

At my side, the company-hired pastor,
trying to pray her into heaven.

I told him she'll meet her people on Pine
Mountain in the brown valley of the deer.

They will sing the forbidden songs.

It will take centuries for the notes to rise.

THE SHAWNEE MOTHER

Before the white man came,
Tecumseh loved the Ohio River Valley.

Green tree caps,
his horse's gentle nuzzle.

Tecumseh means shooting star.

Dreamed of the sky world,
the wingspan of heavens

where the last of our people were waiting for him.

The Shawnee have vanished from Ohio and Kentucky.

There is no singing on Pine Mountain.
The Mad River is empty of birch-bark canoes.

THINGS I KNOW ABOUT MY FATHER

Name was Thomas.
From Ohio, Beautiful River.
Came to Kentucky to work the Harlan mines.
Kept mother's picture with him in the cage room while he rang up and
        down the floors, chirr of bells, always in his ears.
Never took a liking to church.
Gave mother a white gold bracelet when he asked her to marry him.
Had thick black hair that curled in humid summer.
Spent Sunday afternoons dreaming under the Ash trees, plying steel-hair
        lures for trout, birch basket stocked with butter sandwiches.
Sealed in a year before I was born, candle failed, still axed his way out alive.
Got cancer from the coal dust five years later.
No one from the church prayed over his body.
Loved most, fly-fishing the Cumberland River.
Loved the way rain built high waters and surged down the hill veins.
Asked mother to lay him with her people.
Is buried on Pine Mountain.

THE BOOK OF SAINTS

I wrote my name in the Book of Saints.
The French priest gave
it to my great-grandmother during Chief Tecumseh's war.

She passed it through
a century of floorboards.

Father Senet Conte, 1808
Helena, New Shenandoah 38
Abigail Hayes 1865
Mary Garducci, wife of Thomas
Abigail, Pine Mountain

My mother was a good wife.

St. Rita, what charm
do you have against loneliness?

Were you desolate,
like it says in the book,
the night your terrible husband
was stabbed to death
in the Umbrian streets?

Was God's house really empty?
Or only just full of wind?

PIGEON RIVER

After we were married
I took Samuel to Pigeon River
to stroll the eastern bank where the water splits
in two directions
for thirty paces down river
and then meets again
at the roots of a long laying pine,
moss covered, collector of bank silt.

I did not expect him to see the river
the way I see the river,
not the October rapids,
not the gray squirrel chewing nettles.

I was so young then.

How could I have known
that a man of God sees only God
in the water and the stones
and the knotted barks.

That he does not see himself there.

That he cannot imagine himself
part of the body of the world.

BIRTH

You came quick, little sprout,
like spring, and before I knew
what my mother never told me,
your one ruby star brightened
above the mountain.
I could see you all morning long,
right through the sweet bleeding
of the afternoon. Little moon,
little plum. Little one, listen.
The sparrows at the window
are humming
your birth song, that first pink
sweetness is all your own.

CUMBERLAND ROAD, KENTUCKY, 1931

The sun hovers on the corn cusp but won't fall.

Eight weeks of drought. Eight weeks straight
chasing mice from the kitchen.

One lost a head in the drainpipe.

Night sweeps under the dust
clouds blowing in from the Plains.

The clouds waver at the dark horizon but never rise.

VISION

Imagine you have the burden of describing it:
the evening the first deer of the season
is slaughtered and carried home
stick-strapped and oozing red.

The round eyes of the hooked
blue catfish, full of air.

The rough pine scents
the hunter's dog breathes, nose swollen
from perfumes of the chase.

Could you retell a morning of campfires stoked
by the gentle laughing of men?
Of wheats and cattails
that bend away for boots and oar?

So flat the land will look as it is passed
on the march home to hang skin to door.
So starved of the companionship of water
and ravenous for the first boiled bone.

Describe it, now, from the eyes
of the deer, or fish, or dog.

A LETTER FROM SAMUEL'S FATHER

Oklahoma, November, 1933

Samuel,

Your mother is dead.
Cora May witnessed her last coughing.
The land failed us.
Cut the last cattle wide yesterday.
Eyes blind for months.
Belly full of sand.
The soil can't settle because of the blowing
so your mother
won't stay buried for long.
I'm going to California
before she's ploughed up by the wind.
Don't come
to Oklahoma, son.
The Lord knows,
the land's failure is ours too.

MORNINGS WITHOUT MOUNTAINS

The Old Mothers used to say
that the eastern mountains
were the last place left
for our people,
and I think they meant
Pine Mountain too
and late autumn
at the Cumberland Gap.

But I am leaving it.

The sound of the train pounding
the narrow mountain pass,
the black soil and clay pebbles
crumbling around the wood lines.

The damp smell of the ground,
decaying leaves,
coal smoke mixing clouds.

I will not keep fresh
the wild grasses clinging
to my leather shoes.

Nor the bony turkey
vultures, their silent gossiping
on the stripped arms of trees.

Will there be a bridge?

Is Oklahoma a place without edges?

Is longing distanced?

I have spent my childhood gazing
from one rock ledge to the next.

I tried to become the mountain.

This morning when I walked
among the spirits,

the fog whispered down
between the valleys
and I was completely alone.

No boulder to hold my weight.

No tree to cover me.

LAND OF TOMORROW

The night before we left
for Oklahoma I dreamed
of the Shawnee Mother again.
Squirrel-shouldered, gatherer
of angelica and pennyroyal.

We sat mirrored at two ends
of a still boat
in the bass-combed
Cumberland. She sang
the forbidden songs.

Cardinal feathers
grew from her fingers
but the dream burned away
before I could see
red dancing in the air.

BEFORE THE RAIN

I'll never forget the sound
of water crossing the near side
of the mountains.
Laundry snaps, table linens
and bedroom sheets wring
each other dry.
Maple leaves tangle,
enmeshed in browns and greens.
The soft scrape of dirt
and pebbles, and fallen acorns
rolling across the porch.

Or how in late spring,
and unable to see
the darkening
of an already night sky,
the sound was the first
gesture of storm.

Even when I couldn't see it,
the wind, for example, nudging
through the windows
and the drapes leaping
away from the wall,
I could hear the sound
as it settled a chill in my ears.

It doesn't matter how late
it is in coming.
The crescendo eternally
approaches. Wind before water.
The chattering teeth
of leaves before rain.

A LETTER FROM CORA MAY

December, 1933

Dear Mrs. Samuel Moss,

I heard in town that your family plans
on coming back to this homestead.
Please know your husband's father is gone.
I've no family and no way of getting
to California so I'll stay on
and help if I can, if you come.

You'll be happy to hear we've got one horse
still alive in the barn,
and the newborn peahens love
the taste of molasses, and the school
on Cimarron hasn't been stormed
under yet—but oh my soul,
the windows broke out last month
and I'll never forget how far the wind
carried those children's screams.

So's you know, the dust comes quicker
than the rooster most mornings.

Mrs. Moss, I hope this letter gets you
before you leave Kentucky.

In case you're thinking of changing your mind.

Dust

They went in their simplicity, and they knew not anything.

—II Samuel 15:11

SMALL GIANTS

On our way through Boise City,
the only mountains in the distance
are the scattering peaks of a recoiling storm.

The horizon is brimless
but for a rounding from edge to edge.

The woman in town who sold me
the eggs, milk, and flour,
said we were blessed
to come through on a calm day.

I wonder how she could tell it was day at all.

Over the car's spitting engine Samuel barks
for Leah to stop counting the grain silos,
says the house is only thirty minutes from town.

He doesn't know she can't tell the time
without the mountains,
the ranges that divided sunlight along ridges
and valleys, hues fanning out on the road.

Neither am I prepared for Oklahoma.
Nor the hollow metal of the silos,
the grain cars napping on the rails,
the root knees on the bald cypresses,
my belly four months with child.

THE BURIAL DREAM

I am alone beneath tarp
post and wall stone
and ceiling flowers bloomed
from cedar.
Dew covers my face.
Not tears, not fog
from fields, not rain.
Wet of human exhale.

Under that, coffined
where soil is damp again.

Below the crowded grass
blades disowned by spring,
to the air, to the unscreened canvas-
covered windows rising
and falling chest
of my sleeping child.
Below my longing for home.
The goldenrod and wrens,
the mirror clear rivers.

Below the tills I wish to take them,
or better yet, be refused
at the border, back turned
from the mountains
and the calm laugh of cresting wind.

FOR THE BODY AND BAKER

Leah and I couldn't sleep through the first night.
Long after Cora May cleared the dishes
and went to bed, we stayed awake
and watched the sky come with its hungry beaks.
Samuel prayed for rain, for his Lord to provide.

But the sky didn't bring water, dropped dirt,
instead, for hours until morning and night
lost the colors for telling one from the other.

Leah and I hauled a mattress into the center
of the room, away from the windows.

We whispered prayers, too.
Not for the Kentucky we left behind, or rain,
but a song of praise for the two loaves of bread

Cora May forgot in the oven—
the only food we had left that the land had not covered.

UNDER THE BLUE ASH

The fields bloom dying animals—
bones and skins huddled under
the Blue Ash that balds
leaf pods onto the fence.

One cow gave birth at dawn—
stillborn, or half dead.
Something licked the body dry.

The hogs refuse sleep, won't nurse
the newest young
whose eyes are borderless—
less alive than stones

DUST STORM, FEBRUARY 1934

Leah tried to bring the peahens into the cellar. She could sense the storm from the way the cattle shuffled fence-to-fence trying for shelter under the balding trees. The dogs were showing teeth to stay in, but before Samuel latched the door, he tossed out the tiny birds. We can't save every living thing, he said. We could hear their terrified peeping before the dust picked the sounds clean, and the hours after their silencing were the hardest to sit through. After the storm, Leah ran to the fields. The eyeless chicks were gone. She spent days putting molasses on the tumbleweed so the near-dead calves would feed, and never stopped looking through the thistles and taproots for the birds, no matter how many carcasses of jackrabbits and field mice she had to kick through. When she did find them, their hidden bellies still unpicked by hawks, she brought them to the bucket of water I set out on the porch, washed the feathers brown clean, so they would come alive in another world, full of color.

ABIGAIL'S PRAYER

I was a young girl with an ear for the myths
of the wind—
white ghost, cotton mother.

A young girl among mornings
wide with mountains.

I could speak green then.
I could read the water from rivers.

I knew rain.

Those senses stay with you,
no matter which land you die in,
fertile, arid, mountain or no mountain,
those rhythms weld to your bones
even after the body is gone.

Nothing can strip from memory
those seasons of color.

No unending succession of evening storms.

I know the burial ground and a fat rain falling
and my mother below the soil.

How lonely it was with no one
but a preacher

and a barn owl
to hum her funeral song.

I'm sick of praying.

I wanted to believe the music
of the sacred body.

Wanted the skins of heaven.

But when the storms come
and lights chatter away behind
the farm doors
and the noise starts
its stripping of the land,
all I have left is mountain.

FAIL TO IMAGINE

At first, Leah felt like a wing, brushing
the inside of my belly, and before I felt her
hand at the wall of my skin, as if to say hello,
I was sure I would give birth to a hummingbird.

Just a brush, just a wing, as if I might have imagined
her, the feeling simple as touching your tongue
to the inside of your cheek.

But this one is not growing as he should,
has not fluttered his skin against mine,
has been low in my belly for a month now,
hiding from the terrible air. By the time we were over
the mountains he was all bones, elbows, knees,
and my back felt his pointy weight, turning and turning.

I don't know if there will be a space for him
even in this endless prairie. I am not able to imagine
him, as I once imagined Leah, feeding her evenings
at the edge of an indigo stream. Her cheeks soft as tulips,
fine hair curling at the tips, muddy shoes, dress-scrap dolls.
Who will nurse him, if I can't? How will he breathe?
Who will show me how to clean dust from his tiny eyes?

This is not a place where anything new is blooming.
Leah, who once spent the whole day tumbling
in leaves, painting the mountains at school, now ties
a rope around the waist of her torn dress, so she can find
her way back to our house if a duster blows in
while she's looking for dead birds she can wash and bury.

ABIGAIL ALONE BEFORE CHILDBIRTH

On the table next to the bed
are pulled tendons of dried trout
we carried from Kentucky.

Gills are gone, bones too.

A cool breeze eddies around
the dust-ironed curtains,
dries the sweat on my eyelids.

My legs begin trembling,
covered only by the unsunned
cottons I plucked from the line
when my water broke.

Midwife left with the sharecroppers.

No oils for soothing.
No fennel to keep the bitter away.

INTO THE WATER

Leah and Cora May waited at the end of the bed
for him to come through. It didn't take long.

My bones suffered each of his bones.

Cora May has been good with the new lambs,
but couldn't make him jerk or scream.

His arms hung below his sides,
the only horizon for miles.

Leah turned to the window, her small fingers
at the ledge, desperate to plug the gusts that smoked
through the cracks in the wood.

And then he was in my arms.

I pulled back his eyelids and the emerald
stones, like spring, like my father's,
were enough to warm him for a single moment.

And then the washtub next to the bed.
I held him at the water's lip, eased him under.
Too early and green for this brown pasture.

Sacred River, I took your shape for him.

WHY THE DUST KEEPS COMING

Because you have no taro leaves
to pour over the bones,
and no cave for hiding them.
What use for rain
charms when children
drop dead from hunger
in the fields? Or men
from whiskey around fires?
Or women, mouths filled
with a thousand spider eggs
of loneliness? Who is left
for chanting? How can rain
come when the dead
rise, dry as graves?
No stomach from black
calf and sheep. No song
for the dollar-bird,
or pool of water
to drown a snake.
Tongues dry of prayers,
no spit for the sky.

THE BURIAL CEREMONY

The Shawnee Mother came
the night we buried him,
sat at the end of my bed,
said nothing, sang nothing,
not even the low humming
in the back of her throat.
Here in this land without boats,
without still lakes, she sat at the end
of my bed, next to the body of my son.
Her fingers did not turn to feathers.

By early morning she was gone, had become
the quiet walls of the room, his white burial cloth,
the still night free from the shrieks of storms.

Leah showed me where she buried
the peahens, the small mounds
of dirt still sheltered by the hackberry.
Expert at graves, she dug with her hands,
dirt collecting in her fingernails.

Listen, we have learned this—
more terrifying than the storms
is the sound left in the land when they die
down. The silence is unbearably empty.

When the wind came thin as a wing
on our cheeks, I told Leah
the Shawnee Mother is singing—

smoking up from the cracks in the soil,
from the wound in the land.

SO THERE MIGHT BE RAIN

Because the drought endures,
the old dogs start digging—
know what has to be done,
four bony front paws, clawing
the red dirt, teeth moistened
by an unclouded moon,
deep through the burial shale.

They do not raise up
his tiny body for hunger alone.

Three feet of cotton
wrap—easy enough to pull
from the sand—tilling
with their claws until they
scoop out the dead boy
and lay him on the ground.

This is an offering for the rain.

His heart will be eaten
by the summer hawk
circling since sundown.

The worms do not feast,
nor the dirt, will not let
him arrive at the Sacred River
untended by this wild kindness.
They dig around the unearthed
sheets until morning, raw-pawed.

They hear Samuel coming, see the shovel,
but do not run as he beats them to death.

KINDNESS

Leah found the dogs
in the afternoon, three days dead
and in a hymn of sun,
their tails baked into curls,
their tongues leathered red
with the look of stilled panting.

Between them, the young
girl and the dogs, a knowing.

Her dry fingers unlatched
their frayed collars
then pulled the storm-soiled earth
over their broken bodies.

THE JACKRABBIT

This morning is a blossom
of brown,

and I won't clean the porch of it.

I've learned
some things always survive clearing.

A young jackrabbit
warms on the porch step.

I try to nudge him awake,
hear Samuel rustling in the kitchen.

If he sees it, he will kill it,
like he did the mother.

I will never be that hungry.

The young rabbit's lungs open
and close against his rib cage.

Sleep comes only from that steady breathing.

I touch the side of his fur,
which is dusty from a night of blowing
and it seems that our eyes meet.
I want his legs to work, want them to kiss the lip
of the porch and launch him into the nearest bramble.

I want him to be able to run.

I want to nourish the unmothered thing.

Because I need him to be nourished.
Because I need him to run.

Dominion

Experienced people with ample opportunity for knowing
the difficulty of the struggle are advising against abandonment.

—Caroline Henderson, *Letters from the Dust Bowl*

DOMINION, 1935

Leah and I are alone
on the homestead most days.
If morning rises unblemished
by a night of dusters,
and we can see the windmill
past the front porch,
and clean geranium leaves
still pink in the kitchen sill
from their after-dinner washing,
and no grit grates
between our teeth,
we walk out to the barn
past the thistle-downed fences
and try to keep the turkeys alive.

We all share the grains now
though the cattle and horses
get tumbleweed—if they'll eat at all.
Before the sun comes hungry
for the last water in the soil,
I boil the roots for our meals,
for man and beast the same—
there is no more dominion
in Oklahoma. Every dust-torn
throat is raw from swallowing.

TEN QUESTIONS LEAH ASKS ABOUT OKLAHOMA

1. What color are the rooster's lungs now?
2. Can every stain be cured out with salts and warm water?
3. How far can the wind bend the wheat before it breaks?
4. Where does the blood go when my knuckles turn white?
5. What's the name for the color of the rising sun?
6. What dead things get second chances in spring?
7. Will the calves survive another season?
8. Who teaches the mares to lick dust out of their eyes?
9. Does God keep track of everything that's died here?
10. The land curves in the distance, but where does it go?

CORA MAY'S RADIO

I heard the horns coming
from her room on the second floor.
That sweet noise, crackling
static, bolts of voice and note,
and at the heel of the dial,
Guy Lombardo's orchestra cloaking
the room in song. I climbed
the stairs, avoiding the banister dirt,
and when I pushed in the door
to get a better listen, I saw Leah
dancing, a woman now,
scuffing up tiny clouds of dust
each time she dipped and spun.
My daughter, swinging her hips,
cheeks raised, eyes closed,
as if she had found some pleasure
here, and knew it.

THE GULLS

The gulls came to the lake
in a clouded mass of gray
cloth against the sky, came
for the grasshoppers serenading
our first rain in months
with their prickly bowed legs.

Their music sweet and full of shores.

The gulls came to the lake,
which formed overnight
during the rainstorm
that was too fat for the terrace
lines we dug in to keep
water for the seeds.

The gulls came to the lake
and barked all afternoon.

Leah and Cora May
led the last horse to the water.
He filled his belly to its seams,
his happy ears perked
with the song of those gray angels.

CORA MAY HEARS OF THE SLAUGHTER

Abigail said millions of pigs
were slaughtered in late September.
Something about keeping prices
low, but I think the government

men have lost their goddamn minds,
because there's madness in spilling

those pink bodies to the mud.
Young pigs too, and not yet finished

suckling, Abigail said. My soul,
what are they going to think of next?

Burning pits for ripened apples?
Flour barrels set out in the wind?

ABIGAIL GOES TO KILL THE GIANT

The road in the dream
was the road to their Oklahoma
farm, and it seemed almost clear
of the day's hard dust fall.
Opening in every direction
were the black entrances of caves.

A coolness came from their insides
and slow trickle of fresh water.

There was no lake and no boat,
and the Cumberland River
was entirely forbidden.

The Shawnee Mother spoke:

Where are you going, Abigail?

—I am going to kill the Giant.

Abigail said the words out loud
in her Oklahoma bedroom.

You cannot kill the Giant.

Then the Shawnee Mother laughed.

You are already in his belly.

MOTHER OF THE ROAN

A man with silver hair
in a black cattle truck came racing
down the drive to our house.
He stopped in front of the porch
tipped his hat with a *ma'am*
and went right to his work
unlatching the back doors.

It was colder than last year.
Air crisped the last clinging leaves.

He led the mare down the ramp
and she held her head up proud.

Tell Cora May, Teddy come
to settle up on the Gin debt he owe
and that women ain't welcome
at the Legion Club no more
when we playing cards.

The mare whinnied when he
handed me her yellow reins
and he drove away so fast
the dust clouds followed his truck
all the way to the far Ash.

That night I smiled into my pillow
when Samuel cursed the red-winged
grasshoppers keeping him awake late.

I dreamt Cora May, shuffling her deck.

TELL ME A STORY

Of six roans wandering the wheat,
tongues lapping, spitting on cutworms.

Or the mare, card-won
and proud mother of her new homestead.

Of the woman in the black liquor night
of dreams, who arrives every hour
at her home on Pine Mountain,

taps at the door,
tosses stones at the windows.

Of the fields farthest from here,
where even hard rain
can't flood the sweet peas.

Tell me of the dead son
on the cloud tips of sky world.

What song is he humming in his sleep?

Who warms him in a blanket?
Who kisses the lids
of his emerald eyes?

Tell me how to survive.
How the pit of my stomach
can fill with a flower.

STEAL WEST

"...one whose drouth/ Yet scarce allay'd, still eyes the current streame"
—John Milton

1936 was the year the first men started
jumping into cars on the Santa Fe
for a steal West. I saw husbands
hitch out of their stalled Buicks
at the far end of Boise City
like unroped Caspian foals,
leave wives and children with the end
side of that awful train whistle
and the endless rail of storms.

And for what? The camps
in California where tin hutches
wobble unsteady in the mud?

Some of them left out of shame—
unnerved by the killing sounds
when the government came
to take the cattle and the hogs
that were too bone thin to eat,
let alone sell back East.

The women and children?

Most letters have burnt
up now or blown away.

See, there's really no safe place
left to tell a story of dust
and what folks did to clear it.

AT THE TABLE

The forks, and then plates
on the wood, the oiled-over
scratches, dirt-free today.
Leah at the table drawing
a baby jackrabbit, and two horses,
a barn, a mountain.
Cora May filling our glasses with tea.
The curtains, and then newspaper
ruffled from the window breeze.
The spiders at their work
under the archway.

He came down the stairs,
his chest slung with a canvas satchel
filled with bibles.
He looked at all of us once,
in the eyes, but did not speak,
pushed right out the front door.
Hitched to the Federal Highway
or toward the whistle of the Sante Fe.

Gust of clean wind came again
through the screen.
Bloomed geraniums mingled
in terracotta pots.
The bread, oven-warm.

Cora May turned on her radio.

We watched the sunset
for the first time in a season.

Incantation

It was to run

and keep running. Out the dawn side.

     —Anne Carson

SIXTEEN ORDERS AND THE GOLDEN FISH

Bowfin my soul is in that fish
Burbot my soul is in that fish
Paddlefish my soul is in that fish
Brown Trout my soul is in that fish
Longnose Gar my soul is in that fish
Banded Sculpin my soul is in that fish
Skipjack Herring my soul is in that fish
Mooneye my soul is in that fish
American Eel my soul is in that fish
Black Buffalo my soul is in that fish
Northern Pike my soul is in that fish
Inland Silverside my soul is in that fish
Freckled Madtom my soul is in that fish
Chestnut Lamprey my soul is in that fish
Orangethroat Darter my soul is in that fish
Northern Plains Killifish my soul is in that fish

CEREMONY

Evening hushes the farm—
draws down every eyelid
with the auburn sun.

Shrubs, woody vines,
the half-bowed gesture
of the setting world.

The peonies are dying,
but it's summer again,
and their wind-spun dance
is all they know before the soil.

The storms have stopped

though we've grown
accustomed to the dusting,
washing, clearing away.

Leah still inspects
every tin bucket,
washing and drying twice

before letting the lambs
wet their tongues.

Cora May nearly brushes
the young mares bald.

I have become a woman
of the homestead now,

will continue to braid
husks and straw, tassels of sorghum
for my broom.

The day on this almost abandoned

lane, two miles East
of the Santa Fe line

will still begin and end
on the front porch.

I am part of the tracks

that my arms have swept
into the pebble-dented hickory.

This is the ceremony for the land

and everything in it,
which we have spent years
uncovering.

INCANTATION

—after Rainer Marie Rilke

I.

If I cried out, aìn jel eè
would you hear me?

Or the others from the order
behind the gates, fluttering
against each other,
violently beautiful
in your eternal
and inhuman hierarchies?

You terrify me.

You whose name
is inked in the scrolls,
sliced into clay.

What are you doing
behind the pillars?
Behind the black
and waterless dawns
rising along our homestead?

You who know nothing
of our awful soil,
of our loneliness.
You without an imagination.

You don't know what I know—
the plainness
being human allows.

II.

Did the passing
of my first son, last year,
make you desolate—

Is that why you turned
from me, *aìn jel eè,*
and my raven song?

Were you ashamed
for not knowing my language?

That you could not translate
the limp of his body
as he entered the dusty water.

Or the sadness in Leah's
eyes when she went downstairs
to cut a geranium for me.

You don't know
a thing about those geraniums,

or that when you are alone
you must sing of lost women

and dead children,
and past seasons,
and of your home.

III.

I'll sing for you,
of early winter in Oklahoma
when all of the fires begin—
when cinder smokes up

in the rain, when the last
grains are ready for plucking.

For you who are everywhere
and never paying attention.

Let me tell you
the impossible colors
the trees drop along the fields,

and the empty stalks of corn
on the withering path
from the trench lines
to Hawken's farm.
If only you would remove
your golden robes and bundle
yourself in corduroy—
let yourself scab, let yourself burn
with us.

If only you knew
the way sorghum feels
braided between your fingers.

Would you stay in this world
even if it made you bleed?

IV.

Aìn jel eè, what loyalties
do you have for a god
who abandons the land?

I could not stand
to hear the voice of God now.
I have learned to listen
for the sound behind silences.

I am a woman of the body.
I am a woman of the mountains.
I am a woman of these high plains.
But you need to go to the guts
to understand where we begin:
molecules; marrows; tendons.

Because in this brown season
the wind is too strong
to hear the voice of God,
the ground is too hard to count bones.

V.

This isn't a prayer.

This is a homestead
for you of only air—

and you must know it like you are valley--born,

like you have never known a life of slopes.

And anything steeper
than those low degrees flattens
past you, unwinds like a season
along an edgeless land.

VI.

Aìn jel eè
if it remains
that there is no comfort
in this life,
then longing is all I know.

But you should cherish

even the bleakest
of our human understanding.

You are not so far from flesh.

Unhinge the golden frames
and begin your circling.

VII.

You see, *aìn jel eè*
the spleen of the coming storm
is concealed by dusk,

which makes every brown
twig joint seem to dance
on its own against the bark.
And what is strange
is that I want to reach out
for your inhuman hand,

the chapped hush
of my ruined skin
against your glossy imitation.

And not say a thing—

leave it for the evening
instead, when the dome
of stars slopes
the changing aisles of wheat.

You'll know what I know then.

THE WHITE BUFFALO

Came the morning the men left
to scout for food.   Above the sound
of the gallop, we heard the hawk-call
and stopped our drumming.   The fat calf wobbled
up the hill toward the camp, grasses still stuck
to her white coat. No one said a word.
It was not a time for calling out.
She was there and then she was gone.

You are the white-calf woman—
she is in your body, she is in your daughter's body,
and in the eyes of the first and last storm.
When the land needs her, or a dying child,
or the broken wife at the rail, or the woman on the ledge
of the grain silo, looking down, or the calf in the barn
too weak to stand, or the bald hickories at the end
of the lane, she will come, in her own season,
your child, your home, the future of this place—
her white dress flowering behind her.

Jessica Jewell is the author of three collections of poetry including *Slap Leather* (dancing girl press) and *Sisi and the Girl from Town* (Finishing Line Press) as well as the co-editor of the bilingual collection *I Hear the World Sing* (Kent State University Press). She is currently the senior academic program director for the Wick Poetry Center at Kent State University, where she also earned her PhD in higher education administration and MFA in poetry. Her academic writing has been published most recently in the *Journal of Comparative and International Higher Education* and *Inside Higher Education.* Her poetry has appeared in *Cider Press Review, American Poetry Journal,* and *Nimrod* among others. Jewell lives in northeast Ohio with her wife and two gorgeous dogs.

www.ingramcontent.com/pod-product-compliance
Lightning Source LLC
Chambersburg PA
CBHW021201090426
42740CB00008B/1186